SALES FUNNEL OPTIMIZA TION

Proven Techniques, Persuasion Secrets, and Common Sense Advice for Success & Building a $1 Million Business & Improving Customer Journey to Increase Sales

RICHARD N. WILLIAMS

TABLE OF CONTENTS

INTRODUCT ION

In the clamoring universe of online business, where each snap counts and each transformation is a triumph, there exists a little web-based business battling to track down its balance. Meet Grace Thompson, the ambitious founder of the exclusive boutique "Elegance Emporium" that sells handmade jewelry. Elegance emptied her entire being into her specialty, yet regardless of the careful craftsmanship, her deals were a long way from mirroring the nature of her manifestations.

Grace was looking into ways to grow her business when she came across the concept of sales funnel optimization one fateful day. Captivated, she dug profound into the complexities of the, still up in the air to change her striving venture into a flourishing achievement.

Effortlessness began by rethinking her site, the doorway to her gems asylum. She realized that designing an appealing and user-friendly online space was the first step in improving the customer journey. With freshly discovered energy, she patched up the site, guaranteeing it reflected the style of her gems. The route was improved, item classes were coordinated naturally, and great pictures decorated every item page, permitting clients to contact and feel the flawless plans essentially.

As the progressions produced results, the once dreary bob rates started to decline. Effortlessness' upgraded site had turned into an intriguing retail facade, alluring clients to investigate the fortunes inside. Be that as it may, she realized the excursion had quite recently started, and the genuine test lay in directing guests through the deals channel consistently.

Beauty coordinated a shrewd chatbot on her site, intended to help clients in their buy choices. The chatbot, outfitted with information about every item, drew in guests in customized discussions, giving suggestions in light of their inclinations. This additional a dash of personalization as well as filled in as the need might arise.

With a dependable chatbot set up, Effortlessness noticed a critical expansion in the time clients spent on her site. It wasn't just about selling adornments any longer; it was tied in with making a vivid encounter that reverberated with the clients. The chatbot addressed inquiries as well as shared stories behind each piece, cultivating an association between the purchaser and the craftsman.

The following period of Elegance's change process included utilizing email advertising in a calculated manner. Perceiving the force of opportune and designated correspondence, she executed a sectioned email crusade. Clients who perused explicit assortments got custom-made bulletins exhibiting comparative plans, tempting them to return to the site and complete their buy.

To support leads further, Elegance presented a progression of enthralling narrating messages. Each email unfurled a part of the brand's excursion, its obligation to craftsmanship, and the craftsmans in the background. The narrating messages resounded with the clients as well as situated Tastefulness Retail outlet as something other than a gems store; it turned into a story, an encounter, and an objective.

As the messages did something amazing, Effortlessness saw a flood in bringing customers back. The deals channel was developing into a circle of commitment, where fulfilled clients made recurrent buys as well as became brand envoys, imparting their accounts and proposals to loved ones.

Notwithstanding, the business scene is however flighty as it could be dynamic. Elegance confronted difficulties that tried her versatility. Outer variables, for example, changes in market patterns and unforeseen financial movements, took steps to disturb the painstakingly advanced deals pipe. Resolute, Effortlessness embraced development by and by.

She embraced the force of information examination, examining client ways of behaving to expect shifts sought after. By recognizing arising patterns, Effortlessness proactively changed her stock and advertising techniques. The flexibility she showed in adjusting to showcase elements turned into a demonstration of her obligation to consumer loyalty.

The Elegance Emporium was no longer just a jewelry store; it had changed into a powerful biological system where each collaboration added to the client's venture. Effortlessness' persevering quest for greatness in deals channel improvement had supported her deals as well as had made a faithful client base that resounded with the brand's ethos.

Eventually, the story of Class Retail shop isn't simply an account of deals channel enhancement; it's a story of energy, development, and the resolute soul to conquer difficulties. Effortlessness Thompson's process fills in as a motivation hoping for business people, demonstrating that with a sharp comprehension of the client venture, a dash of personalization, and a tough soul, one can transform a striving business into a flourishing achievement.

Importance of Sales Funnel Optimization

Improving the deals pipe is a basic part of any business technique, assuming a significant part in driving income and encouraging client connections. A deals pipe addresses the purchaser's excursion, from introductory attention to the last buy, and improving each stage can essentially influence the general progress of a business. We discuss the significance of optimizing sales funnels and the profound effects they have on business expansion in this section.

1. Improved Client Experience:
Deals channel improvement guarantees a consistent and customized insight for possible clients. By understanding their necessities and inclinations at each stage, organizations can tailor their informing and collaborations, making a really captivating and important client venture. A positive encounter improves the probability of transformation and encourages client reliability.

2. Expanded Transformation Rates:
A very much enhanced deals pipe is intended to direct possibilities through a progression of steps, progressively fabricating trust and tending to their

interests. This designated approach altogether further develops change rates as it adjusts the deals cycle with the purchaser's mentality. A higher rate of leads becoming customers can be achieved by strategically addressing potential bottlenecks and identifying them.

3. Productive Asset Allotment:

Deals channel improvement empowers organizations to effectively dispense assets more. By examining the exhibition of each stage, associations can recognize areas of progress and spotlight their endeavors on the most effective methodologies. This information driven approach forestalls pointless consumption on incapable strategies and guarantees that assets are coordinated towards exercises that create the best yield on venture.

4. Better Comprehension of Client Conduct:

Through the streamlining system, organizations gain significant experiences into client conduct. By following corporations at various phases of the deals channel, organizations can recognize examples, inclinations, and trouble spots. This information considers a more profound comprehension of the interest group, empowering organizations to refine their showcasing and deals techniques to more readily line up with client needs.

5. More limited Deals Cycles:

An upgraded deals pipe smoothes out the purchasing system, decreasing the time it takes for a lead to move from attention to transformation. By tending to likely barricades and giving important data at each stage, organizations can assist navigation and work with speedier exchanges. More limited deals cycles further develop proficiency as well as add to a seriously fulfilling client experience.

6. Further developed Lead Quality:

Deals channel improvement goes past expanding the amount of leads; It focuses on improving the quality of leads. By refining focusing on systems and adjusting advertising endeavors to the requirements of the ideal client, organizations draw in drives that are bound to change over. This increases the number of satisfied customers and ultimately contributes to the achievement of long-term business success.

7. Improved Income Age:

A smoothed out and streamlined deals channel straightforwardly influences income age. Higher transformation rates, further developed lead quality, and more limited deals cycles by and large add to expanded deals and income. As organizations constantly refine their methodology in view of information and client criticism, the deals channel turns into a unique device for supported development.

8. Transformation to Changing Economic situations:

The business scene is dynamic, with economic situations and shopper conduct continually advancing. Deals channel advancement prepares organizations to really adjust to these changes. Consistently examining and changing methodologies in view of arising patterns and client criticism guarantees that the deals pipe stays significant and keeps on conveying brings about a serious climate.

9. Building Trust and Believability:

Customers place a high value on trust when making decisions. An enhanced deals pipe constructs trust by giving important substance, tending to worries, and directing possibilities through a straightforward and sensible movement. As trust is laid out, clients are bound to settle on informed choices and become brand advocates, further adding to the business' validity.

10. Information Driven Direction:

Deals pipe enhancement depends on information examination to pursue informed choices. Organizations can use investigation apparatuses to follow key execution pointers at each phase of the channel, considering information driven changes. Organizations can use this analytical approach to make strategic decisions based on real-time insights, which ultimately results in sales processes that are more effective and efficient.

All in all, the significance of deals pipe streamlining couldn't possibly be more significant in the present cutthroat business scene. From upgrading client experience and expanding transformation rates to productive asset designation and building trust, the advantages are complex. Organizations that focus on and persistently refine their deals pipe stand to acquire an upper hand, cultivating supported development and progress in a steadily developing commercial center.

Chapter 1 Understandin g the Sales Funnel

The deals channel is a critical idea in promoting deals that addresses the client's excursion from attention to buy. It is a visual portrayal of the different stages a potential client goes through prior to settling on a purchasing choice. Businesses can improve their overall sales effectiveness and optimize their marketing strategies by having a solid understanding of the sales funnel.

1. Awareness:

The principal phase of the deals channel is mindfulness. At this point, potential customers learn about a product or service through a variety of means, including advertising, word-of-mouth, and social media. Organizations need to make convincing and designated content to get the notice of their main interest group. This could incorporate blog entries, online entertainment posts, recordings, or different types of content that feature the worth of the item or administration.

2. Interest:

When clients know about an item, they move to the interest stage. They engage with the provided content and seek out additional information here. This is the ideal opportunity for organizations to grandstand their special selling recommendations, elements, and advantages. Case studies, in-depth articles, and webinars are all examples of content that can keep potential customers interested.

3. Consideration:

In the thought stage, potential clients are assessing various choices. They could analyze costs, read surveys, or investigate extra insights regarding the item or administration. Here organizations ought to give point by point data, address normal worries, and proposition answers for possible protests. Tributes, item showings, and correlation graphs can be significant resources during this stage.

4. Intent:

Customers reach the intent stage as they move through the funnel. As of now, they have areas of strength for an item or administration and are thinking about making a buy. This is the helpful second for organizations to offer motivators like limits, free preliminaries, or restricted time advancements to support the dynamic interaction.

5. Purchase:

The buy stage is where the real exchange happens. Companies strive to make this procedure as simple and convenient as possible. Clear suggestions to take action, easy to understand interfaces, and secure installment choices are fundamental components to guarantee an effective change. Furthermore, giving after-deals backing and correspondence assists in building clients with trusting and faithfulness.

6. Evaluation after the purchase:

Customers enter the post-purchase evaluation phase after making a purchase. Here, they evaluate their involvement in the item or administration. Organizations ought to zero in on conveying extraordinary client assistance, looking for criticism, and resolving any issues quickly. Customer retention, repeat business, and even advocacy can all result from positive post-purchase experiences.

Figuring out the Pipe Elements:

The deals pipe is certainly not a straight cycle; clients can enter at various stages and could move to and fro between them. It's fundamental for organizations to follow client conduct and change their procedures likewise. For example, on the off chance that numerous potential clients drop off during the thought stage, it might show a requirement for more educational substance or tending to normal complaints.

Key Measurements for Deals Channel Investigation:

To quantify the adequacy of the deals pipe, organizations use key measurements at each stage. **These include:**

Transformation Rate: The level of individuals who move starting with one phase then onto the next.

Prompt Client Proportion: the amount of leads that end up becoming actual customers.

Cost of acquiring a customer (CAC): the expense of acquiring a brand-new client.

Client Lifetime Worth (CLV): The complete income a business hopes to procure from a client all through their whole relationship.

Strategies for the Sales Funnel:

Segmentation: Your marketing messages should be tailored to each segment of your audience. Not all clients have similar requirements, and customized correspondence can altogether influence their excursion through the pipe.

Automation: Carrying out advertising robotization apparatuses can smooth out and streamline the deals channel. Mechanized messages, customized content suggestions, and designated advertisements can improve the client experience and drive transformations.

A/B Testing: Change things up in your funnel by experimenting with headlines, images, and calls to action. A/B testing permits you to recognize what reverberates best with your crowd and refine your systems in a like manner.

Feedback from Customers: Effectively look for criticism from clients at different phases of the channel. Comprehend their problem areas, inclinations, and assumptions. Utilize this data to make informed changes and upgrades to your channel.

Difficulties and Variation:

The advanced scene and buyer conduct are continually developing, introducing difficulties for organizations to adjust their deals pipe systems. Changes in innovation, market patterns, or serious scenes might expect acclimations to keep the channel viable. Standard examination and variation are essential for keeping up with pertinence and boosting change open doors.

Understanding the deals pipe is essential for organizations planning to drive transformations and assemble enduring client connections. By decisively directing possible clients through each stage, from attention to buy and then some, organizations can advance their advertising endeavors, further develop client encounters, and at last accomplish feasible development. Ordinary investigation, variation, and a client driven approach are critical to exploring the unique scene of the deals pipe.

Stages of the Sales Funnel

The deals pipe is a significant idea in promoting deals that addresses the excursion a potential client goes through prior to making a buy. It comprises a few phases, each with its special qualities and methodologies. For businesses to effectively nurture leads and convert them into customers, understanding these stages is essential. Let's look at the most important stages of the sales funnel.

Mindfulness Stage:
At the highest point of the pipe is the mindfulness stage, where potential clients become mindful of your item or administration. This is frequently set off by promoting endeavors like publicizing, content showcasing, or virtual entertainment. This is about making people aware of your brand and getting their attention.

During this stage, organizations center around giving important and instructive substance to address the necessities and problem areas of their crowd. Blog entries, web-based entertainment refreshes, and enlightening recordings are normal devices used to stand out. The key isn't to push deals messages too forcefully yet to lay out believability and trust.

Interest Stage:

When a possibility knows about your image, they move to the interest stage. Here, they start to investigate your contributions in more detail. This is the ideal opportunity for organizations to grandstand the special selling recommendations (USPs) of their items or administrations.

Content at this stage might be remembered for profundity blog entries, online courses, contextual analyses, or item exhibitions. It's critical to draw in the crowd and give data that assists them with understanding how your contribution can address their particular requirements. This stage is tied in with building a more profound association and persuading the possibility that your answer merits considering.

Thought Stage:

As possibilities show a distinct fascination, they move into the thought stage. Presently, they are effectively assessing your item or administration close to contenders. Organizations need to give more point by point and customized content that features the particular advantages and benefits of picking their answer.

Contextual analyses, free preliminaries, correlation guides, and intuitive apparatuses can be viable at this stage. It's critical to address possible protests and concerns the possibility could have. Building trust and validity stays critical, and organizations frequently utilize tributes or audits from fulfilled clients to reinforce their case.

Plan Stage:

The prospect is seriously considering making a purchase at the intent stage. They might have talked to your salespeople, asked for a price, or started a trial. This is a basic point, and organizations ought to zero in on giving customized and opportune data.

During this phase, personalized demonstrations, targeted communication, and sales presentations are absolutely necessary. Because this information can be used to tailor the sales pitch and address any remaining concerns, it becomes even more important to understand the specific requirements and preferences of the prospect.

Buy Stage:

The buy stage is the finish of the deals pipe, where the possibility turns into a client by going with a purchasing choice. As of now, the outreach group finishes the exchange, guaranteeing a smooth and consistent cycle for the client.

Organizations frequently utilize different strategies to energize the last buy, for example, restricted time offers, limits, or select arrangements. Clear and straightforward correspondence is indispensable to console the client and give a positive purchasing experience.

Phase After Purchase:

The deals channel doesn't end with the buy. The post-buy stage is similarly significant as it centers around client maintenance and backing. Fulfilled clients can become brand ministers, advancing your item or administration through verbal exchange and online audits.

Post-buy exercises incorporate subsequent correspondence, client assistance, and continuous commitment. Giving assets, instructional exercises, and extra worth can upgrade the client experience and improve the probability of rehash business.

It is essential for businesses to comprehend and optimize each stage of the sales funnel in order to increase conversion rates and cultivate long-term customer relationships. A powerful interaction requires constant refinement in view of client criticism, market patterns, and the developing necessities of the interest group. Businesses can create a streamlined and effective sales process that drives growth and success by successfully navigating each stage.

Key Components and Metrics

Deals pipe improvement is a basic part of any fruitful business methodology, meaning to smooth out the client venture from attention to change. Key parts and measurements assume a crucial part in this cycle, permitting organizations to recognize regions for development, improve client experience, and eventually support deals. We should dig into the fundamental components and measurements that shape powerful deals channel advancement.

1. Stage of Awareness:

At the highest point of the pipe, it is principal to make mindfulness. Content promoting, web-based entertainment commitment, and Search engine optimization procedures are key parts. Website traffic, social media reach, and keyword rankings are all indicators of how well these efforts are working.

2. Interest Stage:

Whenever mindfulness is laid out, supporting interest becomes significant. Email crusades, blog entries, and instructive substance add to connecting with expected clients. Measurements like email open rates, navigate rates, and time spent on satisfied pages give experiences into the degree of premium created.

3. Thought Stage:

As possibilities move into the thought stage, giving nitty gritty data and it is indispensable to address concerns. Online classes, item demos, and contextual investigations are key parts here. Measurements to screen incorporate the participation and cooperation rates in online classes, download rates for contextual analyses, and communications with item demos.

4. Stage of Intent:

As potential clients signal expectation, customized collaborations become fundamental. Email successions, designated offers, and customized correspondence assume a vital part. Measurements like change rates from email arrangements, navigate rates on customized offers, and the consummation paces of custom evaluations give important information.

5. Buy Stage:

A definitive objective is change. Smooth and easy to understand processes during the buy stage are basic. Measurements, for example, truck deserting rates, checkout consummation rates, and the time taken to finish a buy offer experiences into potential grating focuses that need streamlining.

6. Post-Buy Stage:

Streamlining the post-buy stage is frequently disregarded yet is pivotal for client maintenance and reliability. Order confirmations, shipping notifications, and follow-up surveys are components. Focus should be placed on customer satisfaction scores, repeat purchase rates, and survey responses following a purchase.

7. Key Measurements for Deals Channel Advancement:

a. Change Rates:

- Measure the level of guests who move starting with one phase of the pipe then onto the next. Distinguishing regions with low change rates helps in upgrading the pipe.

b. Client Procurement Cost (CAC):

- Compute the expense expected to procure another client. Checking CAC guarantees that the costs related to gaining clients line up with the income created.

c. Client Lifetime Worth (CLV):

- Assess the all out esteem a client brings to the business over their lifetime. Streamlining the pipe to increment CLV is vital for long haul achievement.

d. Agitate Rate:

- Screen the rate at which clients quit utilizing an item or administration. A high beat rate signals possible issues in client maintenance and fulfillment.

e. Lead Speed Rate (LVR):
- Survey the rate at which leads are entering the pipe. A sound LVR demonstrates development potential and viable lead age systems.

f. Deals Cycle Length:
- Measure the time it takes for a lead to travel through the whole deals pipe. Shortening the deals cycle further develops productivity and speeds up income age.

g. Channel Drop-off Focuses:
- Identify the stages of the funnel where leads typically exit. Tending to drop-off focuses helps in refining systems and guaranteeing a smoother stream.

h. Profit from Venture (return for money invested):
- Assess the productivity of showcasing and deals endeavors. A positive return on initial capital investment demonstrates that the assets contributed are yielding beneficial returns.

All in all, pipe improvement is a continuous cycle that requires constant checking and variation. By getting it and upgrading each phase of the channel and following key measurements, organizations can refine their techniques, improve client encounters, and eventually drive more effective changes.

Chapter 2 Analyzing Customer Journey

A crucial component of improving a sales strategy's overall efficacy is analyzing the customer journey in sales funnel optimization. A deals pipe addresses the different stages that a potential client goes through prior to making a buy. Understanding and advancing this excursion is urgent for organizations trying to further develop change rates, upgrade consumer loyalty, and eventually drive income development.

The principal phase of the deals pipe is mindfulness, where potential clients become mindful of an item or administration. Investigating this stage includes recognizing the channels through which clients find a business, like web-based entertainment, online notices, or informal exchange references. Businesses can better allocate resources and tailor their messaging to appeal to their target audience by comprehending the sources of awareness.

Moving to the thought stage, it's fundamental to break down the elements that impact a possibility's dynamic interaction. This incorporates assessing the substance and data accessible to clients during this stage, like item particulars, audits, and examinations. Organizations can use information examination to follow client associations with this substance, acquiring bits of knowledge into the particular highlights or advantages that reverberate most with possible purchasers.

The choice stage is a basic point in the client venture, where people are ready to make a buy. Investigating this stage includes looking at the elements that add to a client's official choice, like evaluating, limits, or extra motivating forces. Organizations can advance their deals pipe by testing different evaluation techniques, giving restricted time offers, or executing customized proposals in light of client inclinations.

When a client makes a buy, the center movements to the post-buy insight in the maintenance stage. Businesses can find opportunities for upselling or cross-selling, as well as areas where they can improve customer satisfaction, by analyzing customer behavior after a sale. Using client criticism overviews, following recurrent buys, and observing client care associations are significant techniques for assessing the adequacy of the maintenance stage in the deals channel.

Client reliability is much of the time developed in the support stage, where fulfilled clients become backers and advertisers of a brand. Examining this stage includes estimating client steadfastness through measurements like Net Advertiser Score (NPS) and recognizing the channels through which clients share their positive encounters. Organizations can upgrade this stage by executing reference programs, empowering client produced content, and cultivating a feeling of local area around their image.

Information examination assumes a critical part in the whole course of dissecting the client venture. Organizations can use apparatuses to follow client corporations at each phase of the deals pipe, from site visits to online entertainment commitment to email reactions. Businesses can make informed decisions to improve their sales funnels by analyzing this data, which provides valuable insights into customer behavior, preferences, and pain points.

Another effective method for analyzing and improving the customer journey is A/B testing. By making varieties of explicit components in the deals channel, for example, greeting pages, email missions, or item shows, organizations can try to distinguish the best methodologies. A/B testing takes into consideration information driven direction, refining methodologies in view of genuine client reactions and collaborations.

Analyzing customer data allows businesses to tailor their approach to individual preferences, which is a key trend in sales funnel optimization. Businesses can provide personalized content, recommendations, and offers by gaining an understanding of the demographics, behavior, and previous interactions of their customers. This degree of customization upgrades the general client experience and improves the probability of transformation at each phase of the deals pipe.

Qualitative research methods are useful for gaining a deeper understanding of customer motivations and pain points in addition to quantitative data. Directing meetings, studies, and concentrated gatherings can give a more nuanced comprehension of client encounters all through the deals channel. Subjective information supplements quantitative examination, offering a comprehensive view that guides key independent direction.

Ceaseless observing and variation are essential parts of examining the client venture for progressing enhancement. The advanced scene and shopper inclinations develop, making it fundamental for organizations to remain nimble and responsive. Consistently exploring key execution pointers (KPIs), breaking down client input, and remaining sensitive to advertisement patterns empower organizations to adjust their deals pipe systems actually.

All in all, dissecting the client venture in deals channel streamlining is a complex cycle that includes understanding client conduct, utilizing information examination, leading A/B testing, customizing encounters, and remaining versatile. Organizations that put time and assets in completely breaking down their business channel can uncover significant experiences that lead to improved consumer loyalty, expanded transformations, and supported income development.

Customer Touch Points

Client touch points assume a critical part in upgrading the deals channel, going about as essential minutes where potential purchasers collaborate with a brand. These touchpoints incorporate each communication a client has with an organization, from introductory attention to post-buy commitment. Really overseeing and improving these touchpoints is fundamental for a smoothed out and effective deals channel.

1. Mindfulness Stage:

At the highest point of the deals channel, client touch points fundamentally center around making mindfulness. This can incorporate web-based entertainment presence, internet promoting, and content showcasing. A very much created touchpoint at this stage shouldn't just stand out yet additionally give important data, tending to potential clients' trouble spots.

2. Stage of Consideration:

As clients move into the thought stage, touchpoints become more custom-made and centered. Email showcasing efforts, online classes, and customized content act as key touchpoints. During this stage, providing in-depth product information and responding to specific customer inquiries aids in nurturing leads and leads to a purchase decision.

3. Choice Stage:

In the choice stage, clients are prepared to make a buy. Touchpoints like live exhibits, free preliminaries, and client surveys become essential. These touchpoints plan to impart trust in the purchaser and feature the one of a kind selling suggestions of the item or administration, eventually pushing them towards an ultimate choice.

4. Buy Stage:

The real exchange is a huge touchpoint in itself. A consistent and easy to understand buying process is fundamental to guarantee a positive encounter. Offering different installment choices, straightforward evaluating, and simple routes add to a frictionless touchpoint, decreasing the probability of truck deserting.

5. Phase After Purchase:

Client touch points don't end with a buy; they reach out into the post-buy stage. Request affirmations, transporting warnings, and post-deal studies are basic touchpoints that keep clients locked in. In addition, providing excellent customer support and resources, such as FAQs or tutorials, adds value and supports the customer's choice.

6. Client service Touchpoints:

Client care is a ceaseless touchpoint all through the client venture. Convenient and accommodating reactions to requests, productive issue goals, and an easy to understand support interface add to a positive client experience. These touchpoints essentially influence consumer loyalty and can transform a one-time purchaser into a dedicated client.

7. Personalization in Touchpoints:

Fitting touchpoints in light of client conduct, inclinations, and socioeconomics upgrades their adequacy. Customized email crusades, designated commercials, and redid item suggestions make a more personal association with the client, improving the probability of transformation.

8. Multi-Channel Touchpoints:

In the present advanced age, clients draw in with brands across different channels. Whether it's through virtual entertainment, email, versatile applications, or in-store encounters, keeping up with consistency across these touchpoints is urgent. A consistent progress starting with one channel then onto the next guarantees a firm and coordinated client venture.

9. Information Investigation and Touchpoint Improvement:

Using information examination is vital for upgrading client touchpoints. Dissecting client associations, inclinations, and conduct gives important bits of knowledge. An information driven approach permits organizations to refine touchpoints, guaranteeing they line up with client assumptions and add to an additional productive deals channel.

10. A/B Testing for Touchpoint Viability:

To upgrade touchpoints, A/B testing is a significant system. Businesses are able to determine which elements, such as visuals, messaging, and call-to-action buttons, resonate with their audience the most by testing them. Touchpoints are optimized for maximum impact through continuous testing and refinement.

All in all, client touchpoints are the structure blocks of a fruitful pipe streamlining methodology. From making attention to post-buy commitment, each touchpoint adds to forming the client's insight and experience. By understanding the client venture and decisively upgrading touchpoints, organizations could increment transformations at any point as well as cultivate long haul client connections. The constant advancement and refinement of these touchpoints in view of information experiences and client criticism are vital to remaining ahead in the serious scene of deals and promotion.

Mapping the Customer Experience

Planning the client experience in deals channel improvement is an essential cycle that includes understanding and streamlining each touchpoint a client has with a business. The deals pipe is a visual portrayal of the client venture, from introductory attention to the last buy. Actually planning this excursion is essential for organizations meaning to upgrade consumer loyalty, increment transformation rates, and drive by and large achievement.

The deals pipe ordinarily comprises a few phases, including mindfulness, thought, choice, and maintenance. To upgrade each stage, organizations should initially dissect client ways of behaving, inclinations, and trouble spots. The likelihood of a customer becoming a customer is increased by this data-driven strategy, which enables a more individualized and targeted customer experience.

At the mindfulness stage, organizations should zero in on making serious areas of strength for a presence through different channels like web-based entertainment, content showcasing, and site design improvement. Understanding where clients first experience the brand and what content impacts them helps in fitting compelling techniques. By planning this stage, organizations can distinguish key touchpoints and distribute assets appropriately.

Moving to the thought stage, organizations ought to accentuate furnishing significant data and building entrust with likely clients. Planning this stage includes distinguishing the most powerful factors that lead clients to think about an item or administration. Investigating client input, directing reviews, and observing web-based conversations can uncover significant bits of knowledge to improve the general insight.

The choice stage is basic as it is where potential clients settle on an official conclusion. Planning this stage includes smoothing out the buying system, eliminating any deterrents, and guaranteeing a consistent exchange. Here customized offers, tributes, and motivations assume a critical part in impacting the dynamic cycle.

The retention phase becomes crucial after a purchase for maintaining long-term relationships with customers. Organizations should persistently draw in with clients, look for criticism, and offer continuous help. Planning this stage permits organizations to distinguish open doors for upselling, strategically pitching, and keeping up with brand steadfastness.

A critical part of planning the client experience is the usage of innovation and examination. Businesses can collect useful data by keeping track of how customers interact with various touchpoints. Progressed investigation instruments can assist with recognizing examples, inclinations, and regions for development. Businesses can streamline processes and provide a more cohesive customer experience by integrating marketing automation tools with customer relationship management (CRM) systems.

Moreover, the incorporation of man-made reasoning (simulated intelligence) and AI (ML) upgrades the planning system by foreseeing client conduct and inclinations. These innovations empower organizations to present more customized suggestions, mechanize dull errands, and work on generally speaking effectiveness. For instance, prescient examination can assist organizations with expecting client needs, taking into account proactive commitment and customized advertising efforts.

A/B testing plays a significant role in sales funnel optimization. Organizations can try different things with various methodologies, messages, and plans to figure out what reverberates best with their interest group. A/B testing gives significant experiences into client inclinations and considers ceaseless refinement of the deals pipe.

When it comes to mapping the customer experience, customer feedback is a treasure trove of information. Requesting input through overviews, audits, and online entertainment permits organizations to figure out the client viewpoint, distinguish problem areas, and make essential changes. Effectively paying attention to client input shows a pledge to progress and consumer loyalty.

In conclusion, sales funnel optimization's mapping of the customer experience entails comprehending, evaluating, and optimizing each stage of the customer journey. An effective mapping strategy must incorporate customer feedback, make use of technology, and make use of data-driven insights. By ceaselessly refining and improving the client experience, organizations can fabricate enduring connections, increment brand faithfulness, and eventually drive outcomes in a cutthroat market.

Chapter 3 Identifying Bottlenecks in the Funnel

Recognizing bottlenecks in the pipe advancement process is significant for working on the general productivity and adequacy of your deals or transformation channel. A bottleneck is a point in the channel where the progression of leads, possibilities, or clients is blocked, causing a log jam in the change cycle. Pinpointing these bottlenecks requires a methodical methodology and a sharp comprehension of the different stages inside the channel.

1. Characterize Your Channel Stages:
Begin by obviously characterizing the phases of your pipe. Whether it's mindfulness, interest, thought, change, or maintenance, each stage assumes an urgent part in the client venture. A framework for analyzing and locating bottlenecks is provided by the establishment of these stages.

2. Track Measurements at Each Stage:
At each stage of the funnel, use analytics tools to monitor key performance indicators (KPIs). Measurements, for example, site visits, navigate rates, change rates, and client consistency standards offer bits of knowledge into the soundness of each stage. These metrics can indicate potential bottlenecks if they drop significantly or stay the same.

3. Break down Client Conduct:
Understanding how clients associate with your channel is fundamental. Break down client conduct through heatmaps, meeting accounts, and client venture investigation apparatuses. Search for examples or places where clients will generally drop off or display delay. These subtleties in behavior can help pinpoint bottlenecks.

4. Lead A/B Testing:
Optimization relies heavily on experimentation. Execute A/B testing at various phases of the pipe to look at

varieties and distinguish what resounds best with your crowd. Test components, for example, titles, invitations to take action, and structure fields to uncover components that might add to bottlenecks.

5. Use Client Input:

Effectively look for criticism from clients who have effectively explored through the channel and from the people who dropped off at different stages. Overviews, meetings, and virtual entertainment checking can give important experiences into client discernments and trouble spots inside the pipe.

6. Examine the Technical Capability:

Significant roadblocks can be caused by technical issues. Assess the stacking seasons of your site, versatile responsiveness, and the usefulness of any structures or checkout processes. Users may be discouraged from moving through the funnel if the website is slow or not working properly.

7. Evaluate Content Importance:

Guarantee that the substance introduced at each phase of the pipe lines up with the assumptions and requirements of your interest group. As users struggle to locate value or relevance, content that is either irrelevant or confusing can lead to bottlenecks and drop-offs.

8. Assess the Alignment of Sales and Marketing:

Arrangement among deals and promoting groups is vital for a consistent channel insight. Miscommunication or an absence of synchronization between these divisions can create bottlenecks. Consistently evaluate the handoff interaction between advertising qualified drives (MQLs) and deals qualified drives (SQLs).

9. Survey Multi-Channel Combination:

Check to see that all of the channels in your funnel are seamlessly integrated, such as email, social media, and the website. Irregularities or holes in informing across channels can disturb the client venture, bringing about bottlenecks.

10. Screen Outer Impacts:

Outer elements, for example, industry patterns, monetary moves, or changes in purchaser conduct, can affect your channel's presentation. To avoid potential bottlenecks, maintain vigilance and modify your funnel optimization strategies in response to these external influences.

11. Think about Gadget Similarity:

With the rising utilization of cell phones, it's significant to guarantee that your channel is streamlined for different screen sizes and stages. Bottlenecks might happen in the event that the client experience is thought twice about specific gadgets, prompting a decrease in transformations.

12. Put Retargeting Methods into Action:

For clients who drop off at explicit stages, carry out retargeting systems to reconnect them. Whether through email crusades or designated advertisements, retargeting helps address bottlenecks by helping clients to remember their underlying interest and empowering them to go on through the pipe.

13. Update and iterate frequently:

The computerized scene is dynamic, and purchaser inclinations advance. Consistently update your pipe in light of new information, industry patterns, and criticism. Iterative enhancement is fundamental for keeping bottlenecks from repeating and keeping a high-performing pipe.

All in all, distinguishing and tending to bottlenecks in the channel advancement process is a continuous and information driven exertion. Businesses can improve the efficiency and conversion rates of their funnels by systematically analyzing metrics, user behavior, technical aspects, and feedback. Remain coordinated, adjust to changes, and focus on ceaseless improvement to guarantee your channel stays successful in gathering the developing necessities of your crowd.

Common Challenges

Deals pipe streamlining is vital for organizations intending to boost their income and improve consumer loyalty. Notwithstanding, various difficulties frequently prevent the smooth movement of possibilities through the deals pipe. Resolving these normal issues is fundamental for accomplishing successful streamlining and supporting by and large deals execution.

One huge test is the absence of a clear cut interest group. Businesses may have difficulty producing content that is both relevant and compelling if they do not have a clear understanding of the ideal customers. This can bring about incapable lead age and a reduced capacity to sustain leads through the pipe. To beat this test, organizations should focus on definite statistical surveying and purchaser persona improvement, guaranteeing their promoting endeavors resonate with the right crowd.

Another hindrance is the inability to make drawing in an important substance at each phase of the pipe. Possibilities need various sorts of data as they travel through the mindfulness, thought, and choice stages. Lacking substance can prompt lack of engagement and relinquishment. Making customized content that tends to the particular requirements and worries of possibilities at each stage is fundamental. This includes utilizing different configurations, for example, blog entries, recordings, and whitepapers to give an assorted and instructive experience.

Conflicting correspondence across touchpoints is a tenacious test. In a multi-channel climate, clients expect a consistent encounter as they change starting with one phase then onto the next. Disparities in informing or an absence of combination among showcasing and deals endeavors can prompt disarray and dissatisfaction. Executing a durable correspondence methodology, alongside the utilization of client relationship the executives (CRM) devices, can assist with guaranteeing a predictable and brought together insight all through the deals channel.

Lead spillage is a basic issue that influences numerous organizations. It happens when potential clients exit the channel prior to finishing the ideal activity, like making a buy. Recognizing and stopping these holes is fundamental for enhancing the deals channel. Customary examination of measurements, for example, change rates at each stage, can assist with pinpointing areas of spillage. Executing procedures like designated retargeting efforts or customized subsequent meet-ups can reconnect leads and guide them back into the channel.

An absence of arrangement among promoting and outreach groups is an unavoidable test in numerous associations. At the point when these two divisions work freely, it can prompt an incoherent client experience and upset the progression of possibilities through the channel. Laying out clear correspondence channels, defining shared objectives, and carrying out cooperative cycles are fundamental for cultivating arrangement. This guarantees that promoting endeavors consistently progress into the deals interaction, making a more productive and successful pipe.

Another obstacle to sales funnel optimization is improper automation and technology use. Manual cycles can dial back the movement of leads and improve the probability of blunders. Embracing advertising robotization devices, CRM frameworks, and investigation stages can smooth out work processes, further develop proficiency, and give significant bits of knowledge to progressing enhancement. Saddling innovation empowers organizations to follow client corporations, robotize monotonous assignments, and pursue information driven choices to upgrade the general channel execution.

Improving for momentary increases over long haul connections is a typical slip-up that organizations make. Zeroing in exclusively on quick changes might disregard the significance of building enduring client connections. A very much enhanced deals pipe ought to focus on client maintenance and devotion, perceiving that fulfilled clients are bound to become recurrent purchasers and brand advocates. Executing post-buy commitment methodologies, for example, faithfulness programs or customized subsequent meet-ups, can add to long haul achievement.

An absence of nimbleness in adjusting to showcase changes is a test that can block deals channel enhancement. Markets advance, purchaser ways of behaving movement, and contenders adjust their systems. Organizations that neglect to remain agile and change their channel appropriately may end up losing importance. Consistently observing industry patterns, dissecting client criticism, and emphasizing on the deals pipe in view of experiences are fundamental practices for remaining cutthroat and guaranteeing proceeded with advancement.

overcoming common obstacles requires a strategic approach to sales funnel optimization. From characterizing the interest group to adjusting showcasing and deals endeavors, tending to lead spillage, and embracing innovation, organizations should explore these obstacles to make a consistent and proficient excursion for possibilities. By constantly assessing and changing their systems, associations can open the maximum capacity of their business channel and drive supported progress in a unique market.

Conversion Rate Analysis

Transformation Rate Examination (CRA) is a critical part of pipe streamlining, assuming a vital part in unraveling the viability of showcasing endeavors and distinguishing regions for development. In the powerful scene of computerized advertising, where client associations range across different channels, understanding and upgrading transformation rates is fundamental for expanding return for money invested.

At its center, Change Rate Examination includes assessing the level of site guests or leads that make an ideal move, like making a buy, finishing up a structure, or buying into a pamphlet. The deals pipe, addressing the client venture from attention to transformation, fills in as the system for this examination. By examining each phase of the pipe, advertisers gain bits of knowledge into client conduct, considering vital acclimations to help by and large transformation rates.

One of the essential measurements in CRA is the change rate itself, determined by separating the quantity of transformations by the complete number of guests or leads and duplicating by 100 to communicate it as a rate. This essential measurement gives a standard to evaluating the wellbeing of a deals channel. A low change rate might show grinding focuses in the client venture or the requirement for designated upgrades in unambiguous channel stages.

To direct an extensive Change Rate Investigation, advertisers need to dive into different elements of the deals channel:

Traffic Sources:

Analyzing the beginning of site traffic is vital for figuring out the quality and significance of guests. Breaking down transformation rates by traffic source recognizes the diverts that acquire high-changing over leads and those that require advancement. When compared to traffic from paid advertising or social media, organic search traffic may exhibit distinct conversion patterns.

Point of arrival Execution:

Points of arrival go about as the doorway to transformations. CRA includes examining components, for example, title viability, clearness of incentive, and source of inspiration arrangement. A/B testing various variants of greeting pages can give significant experiences into what reverberates best with the main interest group.

Client Conduct Investigation:

Following client communications inside the deals pipe is crucial. Heatmaps, navigate rates, and meeting accounts offer an infinitesimal perspective on how guests explore through the site. Distinguishing drop-off focuses or areas of delay considers designated enhancements to smooth out the client venture.

Gadget and Stage Contemplations:

The multiplication of cell phones has made cross-gadget and cross-stage improvement vital. Transformation Rate Examination ought to envelop appraisals of how change rates differ across gadgets and stages. Portable streamlining, specifically, is fundamental given the rising predominance of versatile perusing.

Pipe Stage Investigation:

Separating the change rate at each phase of the pipe gives a nuanced comprehension of client conduct. Are possibilities dropping off during the thought stage, or is there contact at the mark of exchange? This granular examination illuminates advertisers where to concentrate their endeavors for the main effect.

Division and Persona Examination:

Not all leads are made equivalent. Sectioning the crowd in light of socio economics, conduct, or other important variables considers designated examination. Understanding how various fragments communicate with the deals pipe gives bits of knowledge into fitting promoting messages and encounters.

Attribution Displaying:

Appropriately ascribing transformations to one side touchpoints in the client venture is basic. Whether utilizing first-contact, last-contact, or multi-contact attribution models, advertisers can assign assets really and comprehend the genuine effect of each showcasing channel.

All in all, Change Rate Examination is a complex way to deal with upgrading deals channels. It goes past a superficial assessment of transformation rates, diving into the complexities of client conduct, channel execution, and the general client venture. Businesses can improve conversion rates and ultimately drive sustainable growth by adopting a data-driven mindset and continuously iterating based on insights.

Chapter 4 Strategies for Sales Funnel Optimization

Deals channel enhancement is urgent for organizations trying to boost their income and convert likely clients into faithful clients. A very much improved deals channel guarantees a smooth and proficient excursion for possibilities from introductory attention to conclusive transformation. In this article, we will investigate different methodologies for deals channel improvement that can upgrade client commitment and lift generally speaking deals execution.

Figure out Your Crowd:
Begin by making definite purchaser personas to comprehend your ideal interest group better.

Dissect client conduct, inclinations, and problem areas to tailor your deals channel in a like manner.

To learn more about what customers want and need, use surveys, analytics, and feedback.

Make Convincing Substance:

Foster superior grade, an important substance that tends to the requirements of your crowd at each phase of the channel.

Use blog entries, recordings, infographics, and different arrangements to connect with and instruct possible clients.

Guarantee consistency in informing across all channels to construct trust and brand validity.

Enhance Presentation pages:

Configuration greeting pages with a reasonable spotlight on transformation objectives, highlighting convincing titles, brief duplicate, and enticing invitations to take action (CTAs).

A/B tests various components, like titles, pictures, and CTAs, to recognize the best varieties.

Execute a responsive plan to guarantee ideal execution across different gadgets.

Smooth out Lead Catch Structures:

Keep lead catch structures brief and clear, requesting fundamental data as it were.

Use moderate profiling to accumulate extra subtleties over the long haul as the possibility advances through the channel.

Execute auto-fill includes and offers clear benefit suggestions to energize structure fruition.

Execute   Advertising Computerization:

Coordinate advertising robotization instruments to smooth out tedious errands and sustain leads all the more really.

Set up computerized email crusades with customized content in light of prospect conduct.

Use work process mechanization to set off significant activities, for example, sending follow-up messages or allotting prompts to the outreach group.

Use Retargeting Procedures:

Execute retargeting promotions to reconnect possibilities who have visited your site yet didn't change over.

Tailor retargeting messages in light of explicit activities or pages saw to increment significance.

Explore different avenues regarding different promotion arrangements and stages to track down the best mix for your crowd.

Center around Client Instruction:

Give important instructive substance to assist possibilities with grasping the advantages of your item or administration.

Make online classes, instructional exercises, and FAQs that address normal worries and exhibit your mastery.

Position your image as a confided in asset, encouraging a feeling of certainty and unwavering quality among likely clients.

Upgrade Deals Pipe for Portable Clients:

Guarantee that your deals pipe is dynamic, as a critical piece of clients peruse and go with buying choices on cell phones.

To identify and address any potential issues, test the user experience on various devices.

Improve on route and smooth out the checkout interaction for versatile clients.

Improve Social Evidence:

To build trust and credibility, showcase reviews, case studies, and testimonials from customers.

Urge fulfilled clients to share their encounters via virtual entertainment and different stages.

Influence clients produce content to make legitimate and interesting stories that resound with your ideal interest group.

Carry out A/B Testing:

Constantly test and improve different components of your business channel to distinguish the best techniques.

Find the winning combinations by experimenting with various headlines, CTAs, images, and even pricing structures.

Use information driven bits of knowledge to refine your methodology and upgrade generally transformation rates.

Customize the Client Excursion:

Make use of dynamic content that responds to the preferences and actions of each user.

Use personalization in messages, item suggestions, and site content to make a custom-made encounter.

Utilize data from previous interactions to anticipate customer requirements and provide messaging that is more pertinent.

Give Consistent Change to Outreach group:

Lay out clear correspondence channels among promoting and outreach groups to guarantee a smooth change of leads.

Execute lead scoring to focus on high-esteem leads for brief subsequents by the outreach group.

Give extensive lead data to agents, empowering them to connect successfully with possibilities.

You can create a more efficient and customer-focused journey that leads to increased conversions and customer loyalty over time by incorporating these strategies into your efforts to optimize your sales funnel. Routinely dissect execution measurements, adjust your methodology in view of experiences, and stay light-footed because of developing business sector elements to remain ahead in the cutthroat scene.

Targeting the Right Audience

Focusing on the right crowd is a basic part of deals pipe enhancement, a critical cycle in expanding changes and driving business development. Effective targeting ensures that the right audience moves smoothly through the sales funnel, which guides potential customers through a series of stages from awareness to purchase.

At the highest point of the channel, organizations intend to make mindfulness among a wide crowd. This is where understanding your objective segment becomes critical. Leading careful statistical surveying recognizes key attributes of your optimal clients, like socioeconomics, interests, and problem areas. You can craft compelling messages that pique their interest and resonate with them by knowing your target audience.

Using different channels for this mindfulness stage is fundamental. Virtual entertainment, content promoting, and designated publicizing can be incredible assets. For example, on the off chance that your examination demonstrates that your crowd invests a lot of energy in Instagram, putting resources into outwardly engaging substance and promotions on this stage can be profoundly successful. The objective is to be where your potential clients are and convey messages that line up with their inclinations.

Dropping down the channel to the thought stage, giving significant and applicable content is urgent. Your audience is considering their options and is aware of your product or service at this point. Fitting your substance to address their particular requirements and concerns can assist with building trust and lay out your image as a feasible arrangement.

Email showcasing turns out to be progressively significant in the thought stage. You can deliver targeted content that speaks directly to the interests of various groups within your audience by segmenting your email list based on user behavior or preferences. Personalization is key here, as it makes a more customized insight for possible clients, improving the probability of change.

As possibilities drop further down the pipe into the choice stage, the center moves to giving nitty gritty data and defeating complaints. Contextual analyses, item shows, and client tributes become significant resources. Focusing in this stage includes understanding the particular trouble spots your crowd is attempting to address and displaying how your item or administration gives an answer.

Executing retargeting methodologies is additionally compelling in the choice stage. On the off chance that a potential client has visited your site yet didn't make a buy, retargeting promotions can help them to remember your contribution and give extra motivating forces or data to support change.

At last, at the lower part of the pipe, the objective is to change over leads into clients. The focusing on procedure here includes customized and time-delicate offers. For instance, in the event that a potential client has deserted their shopping basket, sending a designated email with a restricted time rebate can boost them to finish the buy.

Understanding the purchaser's process is vital for compelling focusing all through the deals channel. Each stage requires a nuanced approach, and organizations that tailor their procedures to the particular necessities and ways of behaving of their crowd are bound to succeed.

It's fundamental to persistently examine information and assemble experiences to refine focusing on methodologies. Use investigation apparatuses to follow client conduct, commitment, and transformation rates at each phase of the channel. This data-driven strategy makes it possible to keep improving, making sure that your targeting stays relevant and effective over time.

Additionally, technology significantly contributes to improved targeting capabilities. AI calculations can dissect huge measures of information to recognize designs and foresee future client conduct. This permits organizations to mechanize and improve their focusing on endeavors, conveying customized encounters at scale.

All in all, focusing on the right crowd is a foundation of deal pipe improvement. From making attention to driving changes, figuring out your crowd's socioeconomics, ways of behaving, and inclinations empowers you to really tailor your promoting procedures. By utilizing an information driven approach, utilizing innovation, and constantly refining your strategies, you can improve your deals pipe and make a more consistent and customized insight for your likely clients.

Improving Engagement at Each Stage

It is essential to implement strategies that resonate with potential customers and seamlessly guide them through the buying process in order to improve engagement at each stage of the sales funnel. The stages of awareness, interest, consideration, intent, and finally the decision and purchase are typically included in the sales funnel. Here is a thorough aide on improving commitment at each step:

1. Mindfulness Stage:

At the highest point of the channel, the objective is to catch the crowd's consideration and make them mindful of your image or item.

Content Promoting: Make important and educational substance through blog entries, articles, and web-based entertainment. This content ought to address the trouble spots of your main interest group, situating your image as an answer.

Online Entertainment Commitment: Connect with your audience by using social media platforms. Share connecting with content, partake in discussions, and run designated promotions to increment brand perceivability.

2. Interest Stage:

When potential clients know about your image, it's fundamental to develop their advantage and keep them locked in.

Intuitive Substance: Consolidate tests, studies, and intuitive infographics. This gives significant data as well as empowers dynamic cooperation, expanding commitment.

Marketing via email: Create an email list and send content that is tailored to your audience's interests. Utilize convincing titles and outwardly engaging plans to catch consideration.

3. Thought Stage:

In this stage, possibilities are assessing your contributions. Give them the data they need to pursue informed choices.

Free product trials and demos: Offer exhibits or free preliminaries to grandstand your item's highlights. This involved experience can fundamentally impact navigation.

Client Tributes and Contextual investigations: Distribute success stories from content clients. Genuine models construct trust and give social verification, facilitating dynamic interaction.

4. Aim Stage:

As potential clients express an unmistakable goal to buy, center around working with a smooth progress towards an ultimate choice.

Remarketing Techniques: Execute remarketing advertisements to help clients to remember your contributions. This encourages them to proceed and helps to reinforce the value proposition.

Live Talks and Client assistance: Utilize live chat to provide assistance in real time. Address any worries or questions instantly, guaranteeing a positive encounter as they approach an official choice.

5. Stages of Decision and Purchase:

Finalizing the negotiation requires a mix of consolation and comfort.

Restricted Time Offers and Limits: With discounts that are only available for a limited time, you can create a sense of urgency. This can push likely clients to go with the last choice.

Clear Source of inspiration (CTA): Guarantee that your site and correspondence have clear and convincing CTAs. Whether it's "Purchase Now" or "Buy in Today," the language ought to be immediate and convincing.

General Tips for Optimizing the Sales Funnel:

Personalization: Adapt your message to the preferences and actions of your audience.Customers feel valued when they have individualized experiences.

Optimisation for Mobile: Given the predominance of portable utilization, enhance your substance and site for cell phones to take care of a more extensive crowd.

A/B Testing: Test every aspect of your sales funnel, including CTAs, images, and headlines, on a regular basis. A/B testing perceives what resonates best with your group.

Investigation and Information Examination: Use investigation devices to follow client conduct at each stage. Examining information can uncover bits of knowledge into regions that need improvement and assist with refining your systems.

By executing these procedures at each phase of the deals pipe, you can make a really captivating and consistent experience for your possible clients, improving the probability of change and long haul consumer loyalty.

Chapter 5 Leveraging Technology

Businesses that want to increase efficiency, customer engagement, and ultimately revenue generation must make use of technology in sales funnel optimization. The incorporation of cutting-edge technological solutions has the potential to significantly enhance the sales funnel, which serves as a visual representation of the customer journey from awareness to purchase. In this period of advanced change, bridling the force of innovation can smooth out processes, improve focusing on, and give significant experiences. Here is a complete investigation of how organizations can really use innovation at each phase of the deals pipe for ideal outcomes.

1. Stage of Awareness: Computerized Showcasing Systems

At the highest point of the deals channel lies the mindfulness stage, where potential clients come out as comfortable with an item or administration. Innovation assumes a crucial part in growing reach and making brand mindfulness. Online entertainment stages, website streamlining (Web optimization), and content promoting instruments engage organizations to associate with their ideal interest group.

Carrying out cutting edge examination devices empowers organizations to follow online corporations, measure site traffic, and gain experiences into buyer conduct. This information driven approach refines advertising systems, guaranteeing that content is custom fitted to the inclinations and requirements of the crowd.

2. Interest Stage: AI-driven insights and personalization As potential customers advance to the interest stage, personalization becomes increasingly important. Utilizing innovation like client relationship the executives (CRM) frameworks permits organizations to accumulate and examine client information. Simulated intelligence driven bits of knowledge can foresee client inclinations and ways of behaving, empowering customized correspondence.

Chatbots and menial helpers controlled by computerized reasoning upgrade client connections, giving moment reactions to inquiries and directing possible purchasers through the data they look for. This further develops client experience as well as speeds up the dynamic interaction.

3. Thought Stage: Marketing automation and lead nurturing technology make it possible for businesses to systematically nurture leads. Robotized email crusades, set off by unambiguous client activities or courses of events, keep the brand more important than anything else to the client. Customer behavior can be analyzed by machine learning algorithms, which can then recommend the best times and channels for communication.

Inventive advancements, for example, prescient investigation, permit organizations to distinguish high-expected leads. By breaking down past information and examples, prescient investigation can help outreach groups center their endeavors around leads bound to change over, in this manner expanding assets and expanding transformation rates.

4. Stage of Intent: Computer generated Reality (VR) and Increased Reality (AR)
As clients move towards the purpose stage, where they are effectively considering a buy, vivid innovations like computer generated simulation (VR)

and expanded reality (AR) can give a novel and drawing experience. VR can mimic item use situations, permitting clients to encounter the item prior to going with a choice. AR, then again, can rejuvenate items in the client's actual climate through cell phone applications.

For ventures like land, car, and retail, where envisioning the eventual outcome is urgent, VR and AR advances can be extraordinary. These innovations not just upgrade the comprehension client might interpret the item yet additionally make a critical and positive impression, impacting the last buy choice.

5. Buy Stage: Secure Transactions and E-Commerce Platforms At the purchase stage, e-commerce platforms are essential for facilitating secure and streamlined transactions. Versatile responsive sites and easy to use interfaces guarantee a consistent purchasing experience. Coordinating secure installment passages and utilizing encryption advances imparts trust in clients in regards to the wellbeing of their monetary exchanges.

Also, the utilization of chatbots or remote helpers during the checkout interaction can address any somewhat late worries or questions, lessening truck surrender rates. Innovation smoothes out the buying system, making it advantageous for clients and streamlining transformation rates.

6. Post-Buy Stage: Client Relationship The executives (CRM) Frameworks

After the buy, keeping major areas of strength for a client is urgent for dedication and rehashing business. CRM frameworks, enhanced with client information, permit organizations to customize post-buy correspondence. Mechanized follow-up messages, client criticism studies, and unwaveringly projects can be overseen productively through CRM stages.

Additionally, innovation works with the checking of consumer loyalty and opinion examination. Online entertainment listening apparatuses and feeling examination calculations assist organizations with measuring client criticism and opinion, empowering them to resolve issues expeditiously and upgrade by and large consumer loyalty.

Consistent Transformation and Reconciliation

All in all, utilizing innovation in pipe streamlining is a continuous cycle that requires nonstop transformation to arising patterns and progressions. From the underlying phases of making attention to post-buy commitment, innovation offers a horde of devices and answers for upgrading each feature of the deals channel.

Organizations that hug and really execute these innovations work on their functional productivity as well as gain an upper hand in a quickly developing computerized scene. By tackling the force of information driven bits of knowledge, robotization, man-made intelligence, and vivid innovations, organizations can make a consistent and customized client venture, at last driving higher change rates and encouraging long haul client connections.

CRM Systems and Marketing Automation Tools

Client Relationship The executives (CRM) frameworks and Promoting Robotization Devices are fundamental parts of present day business systems, assuming significant parts in improving client commitment, smoothing out advertising endeavors, and at last driving business development.

CRM frameworks act as a unified center point for overseeing and putting together client information. They empower organizations to follow connections with clients across different touchpoints, giving an extensive perspective on client conduct, inclinations, and history. This abundance of data engages associations to tailor their methodology, conveying customized encounters that reverberate with individual clients.

One of the critical benefits of CRM frameworks is their capacity to further develop client connections. By combining client information, organizations can more readily figure out their clients' necessities and inclinations. As a result of this comprehension, stronger connections with customers are created through personalized communication and targeted marketing efforts. Moreover, CRM frameworks work with productive client support by giving fast admittance to significant data, empowering ideal and informed reactions to requests or issues.

Moreover, CRM frameworks add to deal viability. Through lead the board and deals computerization highlights, organizations can focus on and track leads, guaranteeing that outreach groups center around the most encouraging open doors. This smoothes out the deals interaction, increments effectiveness, and at last lifts transformation rates. Furthermore, CRM frameworks frequently incorporate devices for anticipating and execution examination, supporting vital independent direction and asset distribution.

Then again, Promoting Computerization Instruments supplement CRM frameworks via robotizing different parts of the advertising system. These devices enable organizations to execute designated and customized showcasing efforts at scale, saving time and assets. Showcasing Mechanization Instruments influence information from CRM frameworks to make sectioned and profoundly significant missions, conveying the right message to the ideal crowd with flawless timing.

Email showcasing is an unmistakable element of Promoting Mechanization Devices. These instruments empower organizations to make mechanized email crusades in light of client conduct, inclinations, and connections. Customized messages can be set off by unambiguous activities, for example, site visits or item buys, improving client commitment and reliability. Leads are also nurtured through the sales funnel by automated email workflows, gradually guiding them toward conversion.

Multi-channel marketing is also made easier by Marketing Automation Tools. From virtual entertainment to web promoting, these instruments give a brought together stage to overseeing and following different showcasing channels. This firm methodology guarantees consistency in informing and marking across various stages, supporting the general promoting system.

Lead scoring is one more significant part of Advertising Mechanization Instruments. Businesses can prioritize leads for individualized follow-ups by assigning scores based on customer behavior and engagement. This helps sales teams maximize their time and resources by focusing on leads that are more likely to convert.

Mix between CRM frameworks and Advertising Computerization Apparatuses is pivotal for expanding their effect. The consistent progression of information between these frameworks guarantees that showcasing and outreach groups approach the most modern client data. This combination considers a more durable and adjusted approach, separating storehouses among divisions and cultivating joint effort.

While CRM frameworks center around client connections and deals, Showcasing Computerization Apparatuses succeed in robotizing promoting processes. Together, they make a strong cooperative energy that improves the whole client lifecycle. From the underlying cooperation to post-buy commitment, the blend of CRM and Promoting Computerization guarantees a predictable and customized insight for clients.

All in all, CRM frameworks and Promoting Robotization Devices are vital parts of current business systems. CRM frameworks give a concentrated vault of client information, empowering organizations to upgrade connections, smooth out deals processes, and further develop client assistance. Advertising Computerization Devices supplement CRM frameworks via robotizing promoting endeavors, taking into account designated and customized crusades across different channels. The combination of these instruments makes a synergistic impact, streamlining the whole client lifecycle and adding to supported business development.

Chapter 6
A/B Testing and Continuous Improvement

A/B testing is a critical strategy in the domain of computerized promoting and item improvement, giving a methodical way to deal with survey and upgrade different components inside a task. In this iterative process, A and B are compared to see which version performs better based on predetermined metrics. A definitive objective is to go with information driven choices that improve client experience, commitment, and by and large execution.

The underpinning of A/B testing lies in its effortlessness. It permits groups to seclude and test explicit changes or varieties, whether they be adjustments to site formats, email duplicate, or application highlights. It ensures a fair comparison between the current version and the proposed modification by randomly assigning users to either the control group (A) or the variant group (B). This randomization limits inclination, empowering more precise experiences into client inclinations and conduct.

Consistent improvement is the general way of thinking that supplements A/B testing. It underlines a progressing, gradual way to deal with refining cycles and items. Through A/B testing, associations can distinguish effective methodologies and flawlessly incorporate them into their consistent improvement drives. This powerful pair cultivates a culture of flexibility and development, driving supported progress over the long run.

One of the main benefits of A/B testing is that it gives clear, useful information. Instead of depending on instinct or suspicions, leaders can depend on substantial information to direct their decisions. A/B testing, for instance, can be used by an e-commerce platform to compare two versions of a product page: one with a prominent call-to-action button and the other with a different color scheme. Breaking down client associations and transformation rates permits the group to pinpoint the more compelling plan, prompting informed choices that emphatically influence deals.

With regards to sites and applications, A/B testing can be applied to various components, like titles, pictures, structures, and route menus. This adaptability empowers groups to explore different avenues regarding different parts of the client experience, fitting it to meet the inclinations and assumptions for their interest group. Ceaseless improvement is then powered by the criticism circle made through these tests, as every cycle expands upon the victories and disappointments of the past adaptations.

Carrying out A/B testing includes a few key stages. Initially, a speculation is figured out, framing the normal effect of the proposed changes. This speculation fills in as the core value all through the trial. After that, the A and B variations are made, making sure that they only differ in the test aspect. The test is then led by haphazardly allotting clients to the control and variation gatherings. The significance of any observed differences is determined through statistical analysis of the results.

In any case, it's urgent to perceive that A/B testing is definitely not a one-size-fits-all arrangement. Setting matters, and the adequacy of this technique relies upon variables, for example, test size, testing length, and the significance of the measurements being estimated. Cautious preparation and execution are fundamental to guarantee dependable outcomes.

Ceaseless improvement, then again, is a more extensive hierarchical way of thinking that stretches out past individual trials. It includes consistently auditing and upgrading cycles, work processes, and systems in view of progressing criticism and execution information. By providing a useful tool for determining what works and what doesn't, A/B testing contributes to continuous improvement. Fruitful varieties distinguished through A/B testing can be incorporated into the standard working methods, while ineffective ones give illustrations to direct future emphasis.

Fostering a culture that places a value on learning and adaptability is an essential part of continuous improvement. It is important to encourage teams to share ideas, gain knowledge from both successes and failures, and use these lessons to continuously improve their work. A/B testing upholds this culture by giving an organized and quantifiable method for surveying various methodologies, advancing proof based dynamics over premonitions or suppositions.

All in all, A/B testing and constant improvement structure a strong harmonious relationship chasing ideal results. As the tactical instrument, A/B testing enables businesses to experiment, measure, and refine particular project components. Constant improvement, as the overall methodology, embraces the drawn out point of view, integrating effective varieties into the hierarchical DNA and cultivating a culture of progressing learning and development. Together, they engage groups to adjust to evolving conditions, meet client assumptions, and make supported progress in the powerful scene of computerized advancement.

Experimentation Strategies

Trial and error is a significant part of deal channel streamlining, empowering organizations to refine their cycles, upgrade client encounters, and at last drive income development. A methodical approach that incorporates data analysis, testing techniques, and a mindset of continuous improvement is required for putting effective experimentation strategies into action throughout the sales funnel.

Understanding the Business Channel
Prior to digging into trial and error procedures, it's fundamental to handle the design of the deals pipe. The deals channel addresses the excursion a potential client takes from attention to change. It commonly comprises stages like mindfulness, thought, choice, and activity. Each stage presents special difficulties and opens doors for streamlining.

Information Driven Independent direction
Trial and error in pipe streamlining starts with information. Utilizing investigation apparatuses to gather and dissect significant information gives experiences into client conduct, drop-off focuses, and transformation rates at various channel stages. This information driven

approach permits organizations to distinguish regions that need improvement and structure speculations for trial and error.

A/B testing, which compares two or more variations of a webpage, email campaign, or other marketing element to determine which performs better, is one widely used experimentation strategy. Businesses can measure the impact of changes and make decisions based on statistically significant results by randomly splitting the audience and showing them different versions.

For example, A/B testing could include tweaking the duplicate, changing the position of a source of inspiration button, or adjusting the variety plot. Changes over time help determine what most appeals to the intended audience and contribute to gradual rises in conversion rates.

Personalization for Custom-made Encounters

Personalization is a strong trial and error technique that includes modifying content, offers, or proposals in view of individual client information. By fitting the client experience to explicit inclinations and ways of behaving, organizations can make more applicable and drawing in connections all through the deals pipe.

Carrying out personalization could include dynamic substance on presentation pages, customized email crusades, or designated item suggestions. This approach improves client commitment, fabricates trust, and improves the probability of change by conveying a more custom fitted and convincing experience.

Multivariate Testing for Complex Corporations

In circumstances where different components cooperate inside a website page or promoting effort, multivariate testing becomes significant. This system includes testing different mixes of components at the same time to comprehend what they interface and mean for in general execution.

A multivariate test, for instance, might investigate the combined effects of altering the headline text and imagery on a landing page. While more perplexing than A/B testing, multivariate testing gives a more profound comprehension of how various components impact one another and considers more nuanced streamlining choices.

Comprehensive Optimization Through Funnel Analysis

Experimentation strategies ought to cover the entire sales funnel rather than just the individual parts. Pipe investigation includes analyzing the whole client excursion to distinguish contact focuses, drop-offs, and amazing open doors for development at each stage.

Businesses are able to identify areas that require improvement by mapping out the customer journey and analyzing conversion rates at each step. Because of this holistic approach, efforts to optimize the sales funnel take into account the larger context, resulting in more impactful outcomes.

Ceaseless Cycle and Learning

Effective trial and error in deals channel advancement is an iterative cycle. Whenever tests are directed and results are investigated, the bits of knowledge acquired ought to illuminate ensuing emphasess and refinements. This persistent improvement cycle permits organizations to adjust to changing client inclinations, market elements, and arising patterns.

Fostering a culture that is open to learning and adaptable is essential to long-term success. Trial and error is definitely not a one-time exertion yet a continuous obligation to remaining spry and receptive to developing client needs and economic situations.

Risk and reward must be balanced when conducting experiments because not all changes will be successful. Finding some kind of harmony among chance and prize requires an essential methodology. Organizations ought to painstakingly focus on tests, zeroing in on high-influence regions while dealing with the likely disadvantage of fruitless tests.

Besides, it's vital to put forth clear objectives and key execution markers (KPIs) for each trial, empowering objective assessment of results. This trained methodology guarantees that trial and error endeavors line up with more extensive business targets and contribute definitively to by and large execution.

Trial and error procedures in deals channel streamlining are basic to accomplishing maintainable development and seriousness in the present powerful business scene. By embracing information driven independent direction, utilizing testing techniques like A/B and multivariate testing, focusing on personalization, leading extensive pipe investigations, and encouraging a culture of constant cycle, organizations can open the maximum capacity of their deals channels.

In a quickly developing business sector, the capacity to adjust and refine techniques in light of ongoing experiences is an upper hand. Trial and error improves the client experience as well as enables organizations to remain on the ball, driving long haul outcomes in the constantly changing scene of deals and showcasing.

Data-Driven Decision Making

Information driven dynamic in deals pipe streamlining is an essential methodology that uses experiences and examination to upgrade the proficiency and viability of the deals cycle. By outfitting the force of information, organizations can acquire a more profound comprehension of client conduct, distinguish regions for development, and at last drive higher changes. In this investigation, we'll dive into the meaning of information driven dynamic in deals pipe streamlining, its key parts, and the effect it can have on generally business achievement.

At the center of information driven direction is the usage of pertinent and precise information to illuminate and direct key business choices. This entails analyzing data points at various points along the customer journey, from initial awareness to final conversion, in the context of sales funnel optimization. By following client connections, organizations can distinguish examples, inclinations, and problem areas, permitting them to make informed changes in accordance with their deals pipe.

One of the essential advantages of information driven dynamic in deals channel streamlining is the capacity to upgrade client focusing on. Businesses are able to develop buyer personas that are more precise and adapt their marketing strategies accordingly by analyzing data on demographic and behavioral characteristics. The likelihood of conversion is significantly increased by this targeted strategy, which ensures that the appropriate message reaches the appropriate audience at the appropriate time.

Moreover, information driven direction permits organizations to distinguish bottlenecks and areas of grinding inside the deals channel. Organizations are able to pinpoint the areas where prospects are most likely to disengage by closely monitoring customer touchpoints and analyzing drop-off rates at each stage. Equipped with this data, they can execute designated techniques to address these trouble spots, enhancing the channel for a smoother and more effective client venture.

A pivotal part of information driven independent direction is the utilization of Key Execution Pointers (KPIs) to gauge and track the progress of different deals channel parts. These measurements give substantial bits of knowledge into the exhibition of showcasing efforts, the viability of lead age endeavors, and the transformation rates at various phases of the channel. By setting clear KPIs and consistently investigating the information, organizations can check their headway and make information driven changes in accordance with expanded results.

Also, information driven navigation works with prescient investigation, permitting organizations to as needs be expected to conduct client conduct and design their procedures. By investigating verifiable information and distinguishing designs, associations can make informed expectations about future patterns and client inclinations. This premonition empowers proactive acclimations to the deals channel, guaranteeing that organizations stay on the ball and stay receptive to advancing business sector elements.

Consolidating AI and man-made consciousness (computer based intelligence) into information driven dynamic further upgrades the capacities of deals channel enhancement. These advancements can break down huge measures of information continuously, recognizing patterns and experiences that may be unimaginable for human experts to reveal. AI calculations can likewise robotize certain parts of the dynamic cycle, smoothing out tasks and permitting organizations to answer quickly to changing economic situations.

Information security and protection contemplations are central in the time of information driven navigation. Organizations should guarantee that they comply with moral principles and consent to guidelines to safeguard client information. Transparent communication about how data is collected, used, and stored is essential for maintaining a positive relationship with the target audience and is essential for building trust with customers.

All in all, information driven dynamic in deals channel improvement is a groundbreaking methodology that enables organizations to upgrade how they might interpret client conduct, smooth out tasks, and expand transformation rates. By utilizing pertinent information, organizations can focus on their crowd all the more actually, distinguish and address problem areas in the business pipe, and make informed changes in accordance with streamline the general client venture. As innovation keeps on propelling, the coordination of AI and simulated intelligence further enhances the capacities of information driven navigation, situating organizations for supported progress in an undeniably aggressive scene.

Chapter 7
Case Studies and Successful Sales Funnel Optimization Examples

Deals pipe improvement is a basic part of any business expecting to boost transformation rates and income. By dissecting fruitful contextual analyses, we can acquire significant bits of knowledge into systems that have demonstrated compelling in streamlining deals channels.

One convincing contextual investigation comes from an online business that executed a multi-step pipe streamlining procedure. At first, their pipe was encountering high drop-off rates after the underlying item view. Through A/B testing, they found that improving on the checkout cycle and offering a single tick buy choice fundamentally decreased grinding and expanded transformations. This streamlining prompted a 20% lift in by and large deals inside the main month.

In another model, a product as-a-administration (SaaS) organization zeroed in on working on their preliminary-to-membership transformation rate. By examining client conduct, they recognized normal places of relinquishment during the time for testing. Through designated email crusades tending to explicit trouble spots and offering extra help assets, they effectively expanded their change rate by 15%. This demonstrates the effectiveness of strategically addressing pain points in the sales funnel and comprehending customer behavior.

Additionally, an intriguing example of upsell optimization is a subscription box service. By examining client inclinations and buy history, they executed a customized upsell technique during the checkout interaction. The average order value increased by 25% as a result, and customer satisfaction significantly improved. The vital action item here is the significance of fitting upsell offers in light of client information.

Moving past web based business, a B2B programming organization made wonderful progress in lead supporting and transformation. They used a content marketing strategy to send relevant and useful content to leads at various points in the sales funnel. This expanded commitment as well as situated the organization as an industry naturally suspected pioneer. Thus, they saw a 30% improvement in prompt client change rates.

A virtual entertainment promoting organization gives an important illustration of fruitful top-of-channel streamlining. They used a variety of social media platforms to spread word about their brand and reach a larger audience. They increased their social media following by fifty percent by utilizing engaging content, which resulted in a significant influx of new leads into their sales funnel. This underlines the significance of a vigorous top-of-pipe methodology in drawing in a bigger pool of likely clients.

In the domain of email promoting, a contextual analysis from a web-based training stage exhibits the effect of division and customized correspondence. By fragmenting their email list in view of client inclinations and conduct, they fitted their email missions to explicit crowd portions. The efficiency of targeted communication in the sales funnel was demonstrated by the 20% and 15% increases in email open rates as a result of this.

Besides, a contextual investigation from a B2C membership administration features the meaning of post-buy commitment. They implemented a comprehensive post-purchase communication strategy that included customized thank-you emails, exclusive offers, and customer surveys after analyzing customer feedback and post-purchase behavior. This expanded consumer loyalty as well as cultivated brand reliability, prompting a 10% expansion in client degrees of consistency.

It's essential to take note that fruitful deals channel streamlining frequently includes a blend of systems custom fitted to the particular necessities and qualities of a business. One size doesn't fit all, and organizations ought to constantly explore and repeat in view of information driven experiences.

Taking everything into account, these contextual analyses highlight the assorted ways to deal with pipe advancement and the positive effect it can have on transformation rates and income. Whether it's smoothing out the checkout interaction, tending to problem areas, executing customized correspondence, or upgrading different phases of the channel, organizations can gain important illustrations from these examples of overcoming adversity. By remaining spry, information driven, and client driven, associations can open the maximum capacity of their business pipes and drive supported development.

Lessons Learned

Deals channel improvement is a basic part of any effective business technique. The excursion a potential client takes from attention to buy is mind boggling, and understanding the subtleties of this cycle can essentially influence an organization's main concern. The way businesses approach customer acquisition and retention is shaped by the lessons learned from sales funnel optimization.

The significance of having a clearly defined target audience is one fundamental lesson. In the huge scene of possible clients, distinguishing and figuring out the particular socioeconomics, interests, and trouble spots of your ideal client is critical. You can boost the effectiveness of your sales funnel as a whole and attract more qualified leads by tailoring your marketing messages and content to resonate with this audience.

A firmly related example spins around the requirement for convincing and significant substance at each phase of the channel. From the underlying mindfulness stage to the dynamic stage, giving important data and tending to client concerns can assemble trust and believability. Content that teaches, engages, or takes care of an issue stands out as well as keeps potential clients connected all through their excursion, improving the probability of transformation.

The meaning of consistent and easy to use encounters couldn't possibly be more significant. If potential customers encounter unnecessary friction or complications, they may abandon the sales funnel at any stage. This example highlights the significance of improving site route, smoothing out the checkout interaction, and guaranteeing that each touchpoint with the client is instinctive and effective.

Besides, information driven navigation is a foundation of viable deals channel enhancement. Businesses are able to continuously refine the sales funnel by utilizing analytics and tracking tools, which provide them with valuable insights into the behavior of their customers. Understanding which channels, messages, or offers are best empowers organizations to dispense assets all the more effectively, expanding their profit from venture.

Recognizing that a sales funnel is not a one-size-fits-all structure is an important lesson in funnel optimization. Fitting the pipe to the extraordinary attributes of your business and industry is fundamental. What works for one organization may not work for another, and steady trial and error and variation are important to track down the ideal methodology. This flexibility guarantees that your deals channel stays receptive to changes in market elements and client inclinations.

Another essential perspective is the essential utilization of innovation. Robotization apparatuses, client relationship the executives (CRM) frameworks, and man-made brainpower can fundamentally improve the proficiency of the deals channel. From robotizing dull errands to customizing connections in light of client information, innovation assumes a critical part in smoothing out processes and working on generally speaking viability.

The example of successful lead support can't be disregarded. Some potential customers aren't ready to buy right away. Building connections through designated correspondence, customized subsequent meet-ups, and offering extra benefit over the long run can sustain leads into steadfast clients. Persistence and tirelessness in developing these connections add to long haul achievement.

Additionally, the significance of a strong input circle can't be sufficiently underscored. Effectively chasing and investigating input from clients at different phases of the pipe gives significant experiences. Understanding client trouble spots, tending to worries, and adjusting your methodology in light of genuine criticism upgrades the general client experience and fortifies your deals pipe.

In the consistently advancing scene of computerized promoting, the example of keeping up to date with industry patterns and developments is central. Advances, customer ways of behaving, and market elements are in steady transition. Organizations that embrace change and proactively integrate new techniques and instruments into their deals channel streamlining endeavors are better situated for supported achievement.

All in all, the illustrations learned in deals pipe enhancement are complex and dynamic. From grasping your crowd and making convincing substance to embracing innovation and adjusting to change, every example adds to an additional successful and productive deals channel. By constantly refining and advancing this essential part of business technique, organizations can draw in and convert more clients as well as encourage long haul connections that drive supported development.

Chapter 8
Implementing Changes and Actionable Steps

Deals pipe improvement is a pivotal part of any business making progress toward outcome in the present cutthroat market. Carrying out changes and making noteworthy strides in this cycle can essentially upgrade your transformation rates and by and large income. We should dig into a point by point investigation of how you can decisively upgrade your deals channel.

Getting to Know the Sales Funnel:

The deals channel addresses the excursion a potential client takes from monitoring your item or administration to making a buy. It commonly comprises stages like mindfulness, interest, thought, plan, lastly, the buy. Successful improvement includes investigating and upgrading each stage to guarantee a smooth and proficient transformation process.

1. Lead Exhaustive Information Investigation:

Begin by gathering and dissecting information connected with your deals channel. Use apparatuses like Google

Investigation, CRM frameworks, and other applicable stages to acquire bits of knowledge into client conduct at each stage. Recognize drop-off focuses and regions that need improvement. The foundation of sales funnel optimization success is data-driven decision making.

2. Characterize Clear Goals:

Your sales funnel optimization should have specific, measurable, attainable, relevant, and time-bound (SMART) goals. Whether it's rising transformation rates, lessening skip rates, or improving client maintenance, clear goals give a guide to your endeavors.

3. Improve Mindfulness Stage:

Focus on making your brand more visible and attracting potential customers during the awareness phase. Influence content promoting, web-based entertainment, and Web optimization procedures to make mindfulness. Guarantee that your image message is steady across all channels, having an enduring impact on your interest group.

4. Connect with and Sustain Leads:

In the interest and thought stages, draw in leads with convincing substance. Carry out lead sustaining techniques like customized messages, online classes, and designated promoting. Tailor your correspondence to address the particular necessities and trouble spots of your crowd, continuously directing them towards going with a buy choice.

5. Upgrade Points of arrival:

The presentation page is a basic part of the deals pipe. Make sure your landing pages are optimized for conversions, user-friendly, and visually appealing. An unmistakable source of inspiration (CTA) and succinct, enticing substance can have a huge effect in empowering guests to travel through the pipe.

6. Make the Purchase Process Simpler:

Reduce friction by streamlining the purchasing procedure. Carts can be abandoned if the checkout process is too complicated. Streamline your site's route, diminish structure fields, and proposition numerous installment choices to take care of different client inclinations.

7. Influence A/B Testing:

Carry out A/B testing to explore different avenues regarding various components of your deals pipe, for example, titles, pictures, CTA fastens, and evaluating techniques. This iterative methodology permits you to distinguish what resounds best with your crowd, prompting nonstop improvement.

8. Execute Retargeting Methodologies:

Influence retargeting methods to reconnect clients who have shown interest yet did unfinished the buy. Show designated advertisements to help them to remember your items or administrations, alluring them to return and change over.

9. Use CRM Frameworks:

Put resources into Client Relationship The executives (CRM) frameworks to oversee and investigate client cooperations all through the deals pipe. CRM frameworks help in customizing client encounters, figuring out inclinations, and foreseeing future ways of behaving.

10. Give Uncommon Post-Buy Backing:

The client venture doesn't end at the buy stage. Offer exceptional post-buy backing to upgrade consumer loyalty and empower rehash business. A positive post-purchase experience is aided by prompt follow-up, personalized communication, and responding to customer inquiries.

11. Follow up and iterate:

Deals channel advancement is a continuous cycle. Routinely screen key execution pointers (KPIs) and change procedures in view of the developing necessities and ways of behaving of your main interest group. Be flexible and willing to change in response to market shifts.

12. Put resources into Worker Preparing:

Guarantee that your deals and client service groups are exceptional to deal with client requests and give a consistent encounter. Their product knowledge, communication abilities, and capacity to effectively address customer concerns can all be improved through training programs.

13. Encourage Joint effort Among Advertising and Outreach groups:

Adjust the endeavors of your promoting and outreach groups to guarantee a durable methodology all through the deals pipe. Further developed correspondence and cooperation add to a more smoothed out and proficient transformation process.

14. Remain Informed About Industry Patterns:

Keep up with developments in technology and industry trends that could affect your sales funnel. Embrace developments that line up with your business goals, whether it's taking on new correspondence channels or consolidating man-made intelligence driven arrangements.

15. Look for Client Input:

Effectively look for criticism from clients at different phases of the deals pipe. Grasp their encounters, recognize trouble spots, and utilize this important data to refine your systems. Client criticism is an integral asset for nonstop improvement.

All in all, executing changes and noteworthy stages in deals channel enhancement requires a comprehensive methodology. Businesses can create a sales funnel that not only entices potential customers but also seamlessly guides them toward conversion by combining data analysis, targeted strategies, and a commitment to continuous improvement. Remain lithe, adjust to showcase elements, and focus on the client experience to guarantee supported outcomes in a cutthroat business scene.

Overcoming Resistance to Change

Any strategic initiative that aims to improve the effectiveness and efficiency of the sales process must first overcome resistance to change in sales funnel optimization. The process of fine-tuning and streamlining the various stages that potential customers go through before making a purchase is known as sales funnel optimization. While the advantages of such enhancement are clear, protection from change can represent a huge obstacle. If you want to see long-term improvements in sales performance, it's important to know where resistance comes from and how to overcome it.

One essential wellspring of protection from change in deals channel advancement is the apprehension about the unexplored world. Workers might be OK with existing cycles and may see any proposed changes as troublesome or compromising. To address this, conveying straightforwardly about the purposes for the changes, stressing the positive effect on general performance is urgent. Giving substantial instances of fruitful executions and the subsequent enhancements can assist with reducing anxieties and assemble trust in the new methodology.

Another normal snag is an absence of mindfulness or comprehension of the advantages of deal channel improvement. Some colleagues may not completely handle how the proposed changes will add to expanded deals, proficiency, and consumer loyalty. Comprehensive training programs and clear, concise communication are crucial in these situations. Featuring examples of overcoming adversity from different associations or enterprises that have gone through comparable changes can likewise act as strong inspirations, showing the expected positive results of embracing change.

Obstruction may likewise originate from an apparent danger to employer stability. Workers might stress that smoothing out cycles could prompt cutting back or render specific jobs old. Addressing these worries requires a pledge to straightforward correspondence, stressing that the objective isn't to dispense with occupations however to improve the group's general exhibition. Underlining the potential for individual and expert development through obtaining new abilities and taking on additional essential obligations can assist with moving the account from danger to a valuable open door.

Hierarchical culture assumes a urgent part in molding perspectives toward change. A culture that energizes development, constant improvement, and flexibility is bound to cultivate a positive reaction to deal channel streamlining drives. Pioneers ought to effectively advance a culture that values learning, trial and error, and versatility, establishing a climate where representatives feel upheld in embracing change as opposed to opposing it.

At times, protection from change might be established in previous encounters where ineffectively oversaw drives prompted adverse results. Recognizing these worries and gaining from previous oversights is fundamental for building trust. Pioneers ought to effectively look for criticism from colleagues, resolving any verifiable issues and exhibiting a guarantee to staying away from comparative entanglements. Making a feeling of responsibility and contribution among workers in the preparation and execution stages can likewise expand their interest in the progress of the drive.

Successful change of the board requires a staged and cooperative methodology. Rather than carrying out all changes on the double, consider a continuous rollout, permitting workers to dynamically adjust. This approach limits interruption and gives adequate opportunity to prepare and support. Laying out a cross-utilitarian group to direct the change and address worries as they emerge can additionally upgrade the probability of progress.

Motivators and acknowledgment can be incredible assets for defeating obstruction. Perceiving and remunerating people and groups for their commitments to the effective execution of deals pipe enhancement can make a positive criticism circle. This propels current colleagues as well as starts a trend for future drives, supporting a culture that qualities and embraces change.

effective communication, training, cultural alignment, and strategic planning are all necessary to overcome resistance to change in sales funnel optimization. Organizations can successfully navigate the complexities of change management and unlock the full potential of sales funnel optimization by addressing the root causes of resistance and cultivating a positive and supportive environment.

Chapter 9
Measuring

Success and Key Performance Indicators

Estimating progress in deals pipe advancement is vital for organizations meaning to upgrade their transformation rates and in general income. Key Execution Markers (KPIs) assume a vital part in this cycle, offering significant bits of knowledge into the viability of various stages inside the deals pipe.

The Conversion Rate is one of the most important metrics in sales funnel optimization. This KPI demonstrates the level of guests who move from one phase of the business pipe to the following. A higher conversion rate indicates that the sales funnel is effectively guiding potential customers through the buying process. Investigating transformation rates at each stage permits organizations to recognize likely bottlenecks and streamline explicit regions for development.

Lead Age is a principal part of the business pipe, and estimating the quantity of leads created is a basic KPI. Nonetheless, not all leads are made equivalent. The nature of leads matters similarly as much as amount. Following measurements like Lead Quality, which surveys how well leads match the ideal client profile, refines focusing on techniques for a more proficient and powerful channel.

Deals Speed is another essential KPI that measures the speed at which leads travel through the deals pipe. By understanding the time it takes for a lead to change over into a client, organizations can distinguish regions where the cycle can be sped up, eventually expanding income and working on general productivity.

Client Securing Cost (CAC) is a monetary KPI that assesses the expense of gaining another client. It includes computing the complete advertising and deals costs isolated by the quantity of new clients obtained. Maintaining a healthy profit margin and ensuring that the cost of acquiring customers does not outweigh the revenue they generate necessitate controlling CAC.

Client Lifetime Worth (CLV) supplements CAC by assessing the all out esteem a client is supposed to bring to a business all through their relationship. Streamlining the business channel to increment CLV includes cultivating client reliability and empowering rehash business. By understanding the drawn out worth of clients, organizations can dispense assets all the more really and center around procedures that lead to supported productivity.

A crucial metric in the sales funnel, especially at the checkout stage for e-commerce businesses, is the abandonment rate. It demonstrates the level of clients who leave their trucks prior to finishing a buy. High relinquishment rates might imply issues with the checkout cycle, for example, startling expenses or muddled structures, inciting organizations to smooth out these viewpoints for a smoother client experience.

Notwithstanding quantitative measurements, subjective information is fundamental for an extensive comprehension of the deals pipe. Qualitative key performance indicators (KPIs) like customer satisfaction and feedback offer insight into the customer experience. Investigating input assists organizations with recognizing problem areas, addressing client concerns, and upgrade by and large fulfillment, adding to higher standards for dependability and positive verbal.

A/B Testing is a strong system for upgrading different components inside the deals channel. By looking at two renditions (An and B) of a website page, email, or commercial, organizations can figure out which performs better as far as transformation rates. Persistent testing and streamlining in view of the outcomes add to gradual upgrades that altogether improve the general productivity of the deals pipe.

In today's digital landscape, the mobile conversion rate is becoming increasingly important. With a developing number of clients getting to sites and making buys through cell phones, streamlining the deals pipe for versatile responsiveness and client experience is central. Observing the Versatile Transformation Rate guarantees that organizations catch open doors from the extending portable market.

Virtual Entertainment Commitment and Impact are KPIs that mirror the effect of web-based entertainment endeavors on the deals pipe. Measurements like likes, offers, and remarks show crowd commitment, while following the impact of online entertainment in driving rush hour gridlock and changes gives significant experiences into the viability of web-based entertainment advertising systems.

All in all, estimating progress in deals channel streamlining includes an exhaustive examination of both quantitative and subjective Key Execution Markers. Organizations should persistently evaluate and refine their methodologies in light of these measurements to guarantee a consistent and viable excursion for possibilities from attention to transformation. By understanding the subtleties of each stage and utilizing KPIs, associations can adjust to developing business sector elements, improve client connections, and at last make supported progress in their deals pipe enhancement endeavors.

Monitoring and Adjusting Strategies

The dynamic process of monitoring and adjusting strategies for sales funnel optimization is essential to the success of any business. Effective monitoring ensures that each stage of the sales funnel, which represents the customer's journey from awareness to purchase, functions effectively. We will discuss the significance of monitoring, the most important metrics to monitor, and adjustments that can be made to improve sales funnel performance in this article.

Significance of Observing:

Ongoing Bits of knowledge:

Checking gives constant experiences into client conduct at each phase of the deals channel. This permits organizations to adjust rapidly to changing patterns and client inclinations, guaranteeing a responsive and client driven approach.

Distinguishing Bottlenecks:

By intently checking the deals channel, organizations can distinguish bottlenecks or regions where clients drop off. Pinpointing these issues assists in tending to possible boundaries and working on the general transformation with rating.

return for money invested Appraisal:

Observing systems empower organizations to survey the profit from venture (return for money invested) for each phase of the deals pipe. This information is useful for efficiently allocating resources and concentrating efforts on the most lucrative areas.

Efforts at Marketing Optimization:

Understanding how leads travel through the deals pipe permits organizations to upgrade their showcasing endeavors. This incorporates fitting substance, notices, and correspondence channels to more readily line up with client inclinations.

Key Measurements to Screen:

Traffic Sources:

Watch out for the wellsprings of traffic entering the channel. Marketing strategies can be improved and resources allocated more effectively by evaluating how well various channels, such as social media, search engines, and email campaigns, perform.

Change Rates:
Screen transformation rates at each phase of the channel. This includes following the number of leads that advance from attention to intrigue, from interest to thought, lastly from thought to buy. Recognizing where leads are dropping off supports advancement endeavors.

Deal Size On Average:
Understanding the normal arrangement size gives experiences into the worth of every client. This measurement helps in fitting procedures to draw in high-esteem clients and augmenting income.

Prompt Client Time:
It is crucial how long it takes for a lead to become a customer. Checking prompt client time permits organizations to smooth out processes and lessen rubbing in the client venture.

Client Lifetime Worth (CLV):
Evaluating the CLV assists in understanding the long haul with the esteeming of a client. Businesses can make informed decisions regarding customer retention strategies and resource allocation in order to maximize profitability by monitoring this metric.

Procedures for Change:
A/B Testing:
Carry out A/B testing for different components in the deals channel, for example, presentation pages, email content, or source of inspiration buttons.

This permits organizations to recognize what reverberates best with their crowd and persistently streamline for further developed results.

Personalization:

Tailor content and correspondence in view of client conduct and inclinations. Personalization upgrades the client experience, improving the probability of change. Use information gathered during observing to focus on and pertinent corporations.

Marketing Automation Implementation:

Tools for marketing automation can make repetitive tasks easier to do and nurture leads at various stages. Via mechanizing specific cycles, organizations can zero in on additional essential parts of the deals channel and give a consistent client experience.

Criticism Circle Coordination:

Coordinate client input into the enhancement interaction. Understanding client assessments and tending to worries can essentially influence the general presentation of the deals pipe. Use input to refine procedures and upgrade consumer loyalty.

Consistent Instruction and Variation:

Keep up with industry trends, consumer behavior, and technological advancements.A pipe streamlining technique ought to develop with the evolving scene. Consistent training guarantees that organizations stay light-footed and versatile.

Contextual analysis:

XYZ Organization's Example of overcoming adversity:

XYZ Organization, a main web based business, embodies the significance of observing and changing techniques in deals channel improvement. They discovered a significant decrease in the stage of consideration by closely monitoring their conversion rates. Through A/B testing, they found that an improved checkout process expanded change rates by 20%.

Moreover, XYZ Organization coordinated client criticism into their item pages, tending to normal worries and building trust with possible clients. This brought about a 15% increment in consumer loyalty and an ensuing lift in change rates.

In addition, XYZ Company reallocated their marketing budget to concentrate on the most efficient channels by regularly monitoring traffic sources. This essential shift prompted a 25% expansion in qualified leads entering the deals pipe, decidedly affecting the general transformation rate.

All in all, observing and changing systems in deals channel improvement is a dynamic and progressing process. By figuring out the significance of continuous bits of knowledge, following key measurements, and executing versatile methodologies, organizations can upgrade their deals, pipe execution, drive changes, and at last accomplish supported development.

CONCLUSION

Future Trends in Sales Funnel Optimization

Optimizing a company's sales funnel is an essential part of modern business strategy because it is the key to getting new customers and keeping them coming back. As we dive into the future, a few convincing patterns are ready to reshape the scene of deals pipe enhancement, upsetting the client venture and, thusly, pushing deals higher than ever.

One of the premier patterns driving the development of deals pipe improvement is the coordination of man-made brainpower (computer based intelligence) and AI (ML) calculations. These innovations empower organizations to tackle the force of information examination and prescient demonstrating, offering remarkable bits of knowledge into client conduct. By investigating immense datasets, simulated intelligence calculations can distinguish examples, inclinations, and potential problem areas, permitting associations to tailor their deals pipe systems with astounding accuracy.

Personalization arises as a critical point of convergence in the mission for improved client ventures. Hyper-personalized experiences, in which each interaction is meticulously tailored to the preferences of each individual, will characterize future sales funnels. Man-made intelligence driven calculations, combined with exhaustive client information, will engage organizations to convey designated content, item suggestions, and advancements, encouraging a feeling of eliteness and importance. Customers feel more connected to the brand as a result of this increased personalization, which not only enhances the customer experience but also significantly increases conversion rates.

The appearance of vivid innovations like computer generated experience (VR) and expanded reality (AR) is set to rethink how clients draw in with items and administrations all through the deals pipe. Envision a virtual display area where clients can investigate items in a similar climate or an expanded reality application that permits them to imagine how a household item squeezes into their residing space. These developments upgrade the general client experience as well as add to limiting vulnerabilities related with online buys, subsequently speeding up the dynamic cycle.

Social commerce has the potential to play a significant role in sales funnel optimization in the future. With the incorporation of shopping highlights straightforwardly into web-based entertainment stages, organizations can consistently associate with clients at different touchpoints along the deals channel. Because users are able to explore products, read reviews, and make purchases without leaving their preferred social apps, social commerce blurs the line between discovery and purchase. This trend transforms social media platforms into dynamic sales channels by taking advantage of the social nature of online interactions.

Robotization, especially as chatbots and menial helpers, is turning out to be progressively refined, offering continuous help and direction to clients at each phase of the deals channel. These shrewd frameworks can answer questions, give item data, and even aid the dynamic interaction. Via computerizing routine undertakings, organizations can smooth out their deals processes, guaranteeing quick reactions and encouraging a consistent client venture. The outcome isn't just expanded productivity yet in addition further developed consumer loyalty and maintenance.

As the computerized scene advances, the significance of omnichannel showcasing turns out to be more articulated. Future deals pipe improvement systems will focus on a strong and incorporated approach across different channels, guaranteeing a steady brand insight. Whether a client connects with a brand through virtual entertainment, a portable application, or an actual store, the excursion stays consistent and interconnected. This omnichannel approach improves brand perceivability as well as works with a smoother change for clients as they travel through various phases of the deals pipe.

Information security and protection are central worries in the advanced age, and future deals channel improvement will resolve these issues head-on. Trust is a foundation of fruitful client connections, and organizations should put resources into vigorous safety efforts and straightforward information rehearses. Finding some kind of harmony among personalization and protection is critical, and associations that focus on information security will hang out in a scene where clients are progressively aware of how their data is dealt with.

Another trend that is reshaping the dynamics of sales funnel optimization is the emergence of smart speakers and voice search. Businesses must adjust their strategies to accommodate this shift in consumer behavior as voice-activated devices become ubiquitous. Upgrading content for voice search, creating voice-initiated applications, and coordinating voice innovation into the deals pipe are fundamental stages to remain significant and open to a more extensive crowd.

The convergence of cutting-edge technologies, a constant focus on personalization, and a commitment to omnichannel experiences that are seamless define the future of sales funnel optimization. Organizations that embrace these patterns and adjust their procedures in like manner will end up at the front of a dynamic and cutthroat scene, where the client venture isn't simply a value-based process however an enrapturing and customized experience.

Successful sales funnel optimization will be defined by the capacity to cultivate trust, establish meaningful connections with customers, and provide unparalleled value at each stage of the journey as the boundaries between the physical and digital worlds blur.

DEAR READER

Your thoughts matter to us! if the book brought a smile or moment of respite, please Consider Sharing your experience through a review.

your feedback is invaluable in making our book even more enjoyable for following.We hope this message finds you well and enjoying your literary adventures! At we value the opinions of our readers, and we would love to hear your thoughts on **[SALES FUNNEL OPTIMIZATION]**.

Thank you for being a part of our literary journey, and we look forward to reading your review!

WARM REGARDS